£1/3<

CUTTINGS 3

THE PICK OF

COUNTRY LIFE

FROM Punch

CUTTINGS 3

THE PICK OF
COUNTRY LIFE
FROM Punch

Compiled by Rosemary Burton

Cartoons by Geoffrey Dickinson

ELM TREE BOOKS
LONDON

First published in Great Britain 1983
by Elm Tree Books/Hamish Hamilton Ltd
Garden House 57–59 Long Acre London WC2E 9JZ

Copyright © 1983 by Punch Publications Ltd
Cartoons copyright © 1983 by Geoffrey Dickinson

Book design by Jon Cleary

British Library Cataloguing in Publication Data
Cuttings.
3
I. English wit and humor
1. Burton, R
828′.91407′08   PN6175
ISBN 0–241–11129–3

Printed and bound in Great Britain by
Richard Clay (The Chaucer Press) Ltd, Bungay, Suffolk

INTRODUCTION

Every week a sacred ritual takes place in the *Punch* office as someone skilled with a knife opens the pile of envelopes addressed to the Country Life column and carefully decants the precious contents. Many of the cuttings sent to *Punch* have travelled great distances. Yellowed under a tropical sun, doused by the Monsoon, fragile after their arduous journey from Papua New Guinea or Purley, they must be handled with care. Sometimes it is necessary to unfold a whole newspaper and scan several pages for the small item ringed in red. More often a tiny scrap of newsprint lurks at the bottom of an otherwise empty envelope – one ill-timed sneeze and it could be lost forever.

A Country Life snippet deals with some item of news overlooked by the national papers. It may be something straightforward, rendered ridiculous by a misprint; it may result from the unwise juxtaposition of two unrelated stories; it may just be idiotic or highly improbable. Above all, the humour must be unintentional. One thing is certain: the true Country Life cutting defies definition. So, here, instead of definitions, are several hundred of the best examples from the latest issues of *Punch*.

Hunter Tripod 3 legs, never used.

J. Collins *(The Job)*

Speedy Fit Exhausts is now under the new management of Eddie Rust.

D. Cresswell *(Shrewsbury Admag)*

Old-fashioned fur coats from £50—Clacton Dog Rescue, Clacton.

R. Cantrell *(Colchester Evening Gazette)*

Let us all have a good start to telephone manners for 1983. That applies to those who make obscene calls as well.

D. Wood *(Zimbabwe Herald)*

The term "Passion" in a Christian context refers to the traffic experiences of Christ in the last few days of his life.

B. Whelan *(Farnham Herald)*

Last year the council took the seats away and the problem of drunks disappeared. Then new "drunk proof" seats were provided, designed so that drunks would fall off.

T. Dodd *(Oxford Times)*

Today with our many modern conveniences and push bottom lifestyle, the extra attention to details that woodburning requires are quite often ignored.

D. Campbell *(Bancroft Times, Ontario)*

The trees and bushes in Great Bromley and Frating will soon be painted blue, if parish councillors get their way.

Frating Parish Council wants to see the countryside blend in with a 12,000 square feet commercial vehicle workshop which has been painted bright blue.

M. Ennals *(Essex County Standard)*

Interpreting the mosaics is a job for an expert, but even a layman can see that some are black and white, while others are beautifully coloured.

R. Saunderson *(West Sussex Gazette)*

The duo of Jan Wentworth as Rosalie and Pat Moors as the domineering Madame Rosepetal went so well that one moment one could hear a pin drop at another there was not a dry seat in the auditorium.

M. Lees *(Sunday Times of Zambia)*

MAN 45, 6′ 2″, fed up with being one of the boys, wishes to meet woman 40–50 who feels the same.

G. Melio (*Beckenham and Penge News*)

After a 40,000 miles trip around the world's main cities, 20-year-old Belinda Green, this year's Miss World visited Tottenham Mecca Bingo Social Club.

D. Stead (*Tottenham and Wood Green Weekly Herald*)

A quarter of all households in Kingston contains one or more pensioners living alone.

R. Burke (*The Kingston Informer*)

Widower 52, a lonely sincere genuine man who is certainly not at the pope and slippers stage of life.

M. Davis (*Toowoomba, Queensland Chronicle*)

If islanders agree, tourist chiefs are planning to launch a campaign promoting Islay as a healthy haven for tired tycoons from all over the world. The last time Islay made headlines was when it had a big outbreak of salmonella food poisoning last year.

J. Sadek (*Birmingham Evening Mail*)

A Felling man who almost strangled his estranged wife to death was given a second chance by a judge last week.

J. Irwin (*Gateshead Post*)

A pet shop in South Farm Road, Worthing, can become a Chinese takeaway, Worthing planners agreed.

L. Malaws (*Brighton Evening Argus*)

Boil for one minute all water for drinking and food preparation. If water contains sediment, let it stand, then strain through clean muslim before boiling.

A. Parsons (*Hereford Times*)

Pedestrians crossing Stanningley Road at the junction of Armley Lodge Road and Branch Road at 9.30 today said the sausages had not been there at seven.

S. Gardiner (*Yorkshire Evening Post*)

Perhaps more people will realise that agorophobia is not just a figment of the imagination now. It's time that the complaint was brought out into the open.

G. Burkinshaw (*Barnsley Chronicle*)

We all know that the stimulant effects of coffee are due to caffeine, and that this acts by inhibiting the enzyme cyclic nucleotide phosphodiesterase, thus enhancing the various effects mediated by this ubiquitous intracellular second messenger. Or that was what we thought we knew.

J. Fremlin (*Nature*)

Two men are helping the police with inquiries into the near-wrecking of the new "vandal-proof" phone boxes at St Ouen, Gorey and Havre des Pas—boxes which have now been redesignated "vandal-resistant".

A. Taylor (*Jersey Evening Post*)

Conservative Leader Coun David Heslop queried a recent British Rail claim that return trains sometimes ran late because the distance from London to Sheffield was slightly longer than the distance from Sheffield to London.

P. Rolfe (*Sheffield Morning Telegraph*)

CORRECTION. Due to an inverted headline, a court report in last week's "Weekly News" was headed "Greaser hit Mod in the face after threat."
   This should have read: "Mod hit Greaser in the face after threat."

M. Stevens (*Saffron Walden Weekly News*)

St. Andrew's Church forms an elegant background to excavations for the new main sewer in Cheltenham.

D. Hall (*Gloucestershire Echo*)

"No wonder there are many crimes in this province because most of them are committed by policemen and this makes investigations in the cases very difficult," the judge said.
   Although they were charged with two counts "they will only hang once," he said.

O. Irwin (*Times of Zambia*)

Remember, a cold takes two weeks to go completely but only a fortnight if you take medicine.

W. Horton (*County Border News, Sevenoaks*)

The main differences between the Baptist Church in England and Australia were because there were Australians in one country and English people in the other, the recently appointed minister of the Hughes Baptist Church, the Reverend Roger Bacon, said.

R. Watkins (*Canberra Times*)

Mr Bloomingdale, who died of cancer on August 20, aged 66, had promised her lifetime support and a home in return for devoting all of her time to him.

She said that for the 12 years preceding his death she kept her part of the promise, except for brief periods when she was married to three other men.

J. McKenzie *(New Zealand Herald)*

They gave the go-ahead this week to take a positive lead in felling and treating all dead elms seriously affected by the disease on their own property and to take steps to ensure that owners of dead or dying trees also be felled and destroyed.

H. Henderson *(Musselburgh News)*

A man was fined £150 and disqualified from driving for having excess blood in his alcohol.

C. Cleaver *(Mid Sussex Times)*

Bangor Cathedral choir, the only Welsh choir invited to sing at the Worms International Symposium in Germany this July, needs between £3,000 and £4,000 to pay for the tripe.

H. Ridler *(North Wales Chronicle)*

Bathroom dancing Partner needed, mature, unattached lady interested in medal and/or social for gentleman in 50s.

D. Gray *(Birmingham Evening Mail)*

At the markets, the price of a bunch of chomolier leaves which are tied in tens remained the same at 10 ngwee. But the number of leaves has been reduced from 10 to five.

J. Watts *(Zambia Daily Mail)*

DRESS UP CRAZY! BE DIFFERENT! Let your imagination run wild! Gents please wear jackets—No denims, T-shirts or training shoes.

J. Weston *(Cambridge Town Crier)*

SNOW REPORT Cairngorm—No report because of bad weather.

F. McAdams *(Glasgow Herald)*

Open Nightly for table reservations. The customer seeking the best of international cuisine will be disappointed.

T. Shearman *(The Penwith Pirate)*

Mr Leach said: "It was a somewhat unusual forgery. One side represented a £5 note and the other £10."

J. Hopkins *(Birmingham Evening Mail)*

The elderly residents of Wilkinson House, Peckham, London, ignored orders to lie on the floor and some brandished their walking sticks until the raiders fled empty-handed.

Mr Anthony Birch, director of the home said: "Half the residents couldn't hear a word the raiders were saying because they had their hearing aids tuned to Radio Two."

R. Sandeman *(The Scotsman)*

"I hope for peace—real peace and progress towards multilateral nuclear war."

I. Bryers *(Adscene, Kent)*

A spokesman for Ind Coope said: "This ale is being produced as close as possible to the original recipe which, unfortunately, we couldn't find."

G. Kelly *(Edinburgh Evening News)*

To claim that teachers are in the beer gardens by 10 am is a gross exaggeration, since the headmaster and his deputies are always there to discipline staff who do so.

D. Michie *(Zimbabwe Sunday Mail)*

Penryn Reserves, who had beaten Penryn Reserves on two previous occasions, failed to make it a hat-trick of victories when they were beaten by a single point.

R. Bolitho *(Falmouth Packet)*

The British were reminded that the White Cliffs of Dover at Land's End are the very last point in Britain from which one can gaze out over the vast seas towards unseen America—if one so wishes.

R. Langford *(New Zealand Woman's Weekly)*

They sat round the table and talked. As well as telling lurid tales about World War I perhaps they spoke about the riots at Luton peace celebrations.

J. Hamblin *(St Albans Review)*

A circular saw operator lost his job when his employers discovered he had been registered blind for three years, an industrial tribunal in Birmingham heard yesterday.

A. Elshout *(Birmingham Post)*

Meanwhile, Mr Michael Brown of the Endemic Diseases Control Unit, has told the Justice O. B. R. Tejan commission in Bo that fingerprints which appeared on 44 vouchers were not made by hand but were in fact toe-printed by a temporary clerk at the Unit using his big toe.

A. Davies *(West Africa)*

Mr Brian Campbell said that hopefully most golfers played golf more than once, whereas it was highly unlikely a person would be cremated more than once, so the two were not comparable.

J. Greaves *(Newcastle-under-Lyme Evening Sentinel)*

ANNUAL MEETING of the Society of Clairvoyance has been cancelled due to unforeseen circumstances.

M. Shanker *(Daily O'Collegian, Stillwater, Oklahoma)*

In one of his last acts before leaving office, Gov. William P. Clements Jr. this week declared an Armadillo Safety Day and asked that people try not to run over armadillos with their cars.

R. McCormick *(Dallas Times Herald)*

RULES OF ENTRY. 2. Responsibility cannot be accepted for entries lost, damaged or delayed in transit to the competition address. This competition is organised by The Post Office.

M. Miller *(Post-A-Book Competition leaflet)*

And Stein has also recently chosen Hamish McAlpine, of Dundee United, to keep goal for the Scotland Under-21 side. McAlpine will be 35 in January.

A. Gillespie *(The Scotsman)*

"They should be detained under the Prevention of Tourism Act, and then shipped back to where they came from."

J. Bayly *(Portsmouth News)*

It is understood that the combined Falcon/Plumtree team, who are also touring the UK, lost their first match 0–6 in thick fog. However, it is not known who their opposition was.

R. Lewis *(Zimbabwe Herald)*

Other pieces during the evening include the Piano Quartet E Flat major k493 by Mozart and Walton's two pieces for lion and piano.

E. Friend *(Sale and Altrincham Messenger)*

Wayne Orpwood (23) is recovering in hospital after being bitten by a German shepherd dog making a door-to-door collection for the Society for the Prevention of Cruelty to Animals.

D. Zwart *(West Australian)*

FOR SALE. Man's Gannex mackintosh, length 42″, good condition, slightly dirty.

A. Tarrant *(Cambridge Town Crier)*

"We are totally at one in saying that the essence of begging is asking for money," said the judge.

R. Bladen (*Manchester Evening News*)

SLAIN MAN IN LINGERIE EATEN BY DOG.

B. Walker (*Detroit Free Press*)

The recipe for Scotch Oat Cakes should have read 3 cups of rolled oats and not 3 cwts.

A. Nesbit (*Aylesbury Parish Magazine*)

But even the most careful game plan can be upset by chance. It probably won't happen to you or your spouse, but what if you were to die before you were able to complete your Individual Retirement Account program? Untimely death could have a serious effect on the retirement lifestyle you've planned.

P. Barna (*Fidelity Federal newsletter*)

MERCY DASH TO HOSPITAL ENDS LAUNDRY CRISIS

T. Adam (*Eastern Evening News*)

Deputy organist of St John's Bexley, Mrs Margaret Bearfoot said she objected strongly to being recorded without her knowledge, particularly as it put her off.

G. Warne (*Kentish Times*)

CONCERTS. Ulster Orchestra. Beethoven Night. Mendelssohn's Elijah.

G. Myers (*Belfast Telegraph*)

A chance in a lifetime! This IS unbeatable! We now offer "brand new" Otto Bach, Dietmann or Gors & Kallmann South African assembled pianos with above German sounding names.

T. Bowen (*South Africa Evening Post*)

In the middle 1960s he was diagnosed schizophrenic and committed to two Missouri health centres.

D. Weber-Wulff (*Stars and Stripes*)

Sir, Although very moderate and reasonable about politics, I do not agree with Mr Nott about cutting the Navy. We are an island and not self supporting. Also, where would we be now if it had not been for Noah's Ark?

R. Coker (*Northavon Gazette*)

Although he comes from Gloucester he's no stranger to Liverpool, having been born and brought up in Manchester.

F. Molyneux (*Radio Times North West*)

The school is presently sited on about five acres of steep land, and has 445 children on the roll.

T. Porter (*Lillydale & Yarra Valley Express*)

"When I eventually complete my studies I hope to specialise in sports injuries. That will be my way of putting something back into rugby in return for what I have received from it."

R. Harmer (*Johannesburg Sunday Times*)

Her husband has had the plaster removed from the leg he injured when he slipped while entering the town hall by the entrance for disabled people.

R. Bladen (*Manchester Evening News*)

Pets sprayed, competitive rates, any colour or finish.

M. Clark (*County Border News*)

A father and son were both stabbed as fighting with knives and wooden clubs broke out at the Syrian Orthodox Church in the Sydney suburb of Lidcombe, on Sunday. Police had to be called to break up the fight which spread into the churchyard. They said the battle had been caused by several families feuding over who should pass around the collection plate.

R. Sawkins (*Brisbane Courier-Mail*)

A group of 43 retired gardeners and their wives or widows had a week beside the seaside last month—courtesy of a charity.

J. Anderson (*Amateur Gardening*)

A 32-year-old Clackmannan man, who has already been banned for life from driving, was banned for an additional five years at Perth Sheriff Court yesterday.

V. Reid (*Dundee Courier and Advertiser*)

Diaz said someone from the neighborhood probably is the killer because public transportation is not good in the area.

G. Carroll (*Cleveland, Ohio Plain Dealer*)

United fans can still hardly get used to the idea of Keegan in a black and white skirt but the thoughts of losing their new idol after 12 months must be frightening.

R. McLeod (*Evening Chronicle, Newcastle*)

When the Romans founded their most northerly outpost in North-West England in AD 82, they could have had not the slightest idea that 1,900 years later a BBC orchestra from Scotland would have an important part in the *Carlisle 1900* celebrations.

A. Sutherland (*Radio Times*)

Professional writer Mrs Cohen went on: "We have found that many of the problems encountered by old people in Florida and Southend are similar—although different."

C. Rosenberg (*Yellow Advertiser, Southend*)

Improving Industrial Relations in the NHS—Item 724 (b). It was noted that the two seminars which had been arranged on this item had been deferred owing to industrial action.

M. Green (*Minutes—NALGO meeting*)

Brighton magistrates have granted two bar extensions for the conference of Alcoholics Anonymous at the sea-front conference centre.

A. Howard (*Portsmouth Evening Echo*)

Can you read? If not, phone 21167.

M. Bond (*What's On In and Around Faringdon*)

A Zimbabwean journalist colleague showed us a note circulated from his editor which stipulates that on no account must reporters write that talks held between President Canaan Banana and other dignitaries were "fruitful".

T. Wall (*Times of Zambia*)

A youth stole a shirt from Littlewoods, Lincoln, so that he could look smart when he appeared in court the next day, the city magistrates were told.

R. Lidbetter (*Lincolnshire Echo*)

ROMAN CATHOLICS
There are 12,00 Roman Catholics in the state of Kentucky, one for every, man, woman and child.

Anon (*Village Voice*)

Broken windows at the Carr Hill Clinic have been replaced with toughened glass to try and minimise future breakages. But after the special glass went in, a mother complained to clinic staff that it had caused an injury to her son's head. Her son, she said, had received a cut head when a piece of brick he had hurled at a window bounced back from the toughened glass and struck him.

S. Gilley (*Gateshead Post*)

Are you depressed? Lonely? Sick? Come and see that Jesus Christ is the same. Assembly of God Church, Mount Pleasant.

A. Salmon *(Kent & Sussex Courier)*

An 80-year old Broadmayne man did a U-turn in a main road near his home and collided with a motor cycle, causing thousands of pounds worth of damage and slight injuries. But after a plea from his solicitor, the magistrates decided Aubrey Frank Waterman should not be disqualified until he passes a driving test.

J. Ryan *(Weymouth Evening Echo)*

Supt. John Riordan said the defendant collided with an oncoming vehicle. At the time the defendant was completely on his incorrect side of the road, but would have been on his correct side had he been in Germany.

T. Edbrooke *(Irish Press)*

No spokesman from the county council's Land and Buildings Department was available for comment today. A council information officer said that all the senior officials in the department were attending a course on how to deal with Press inquiries.

J. Benson *(Cambridge Evening News)*

Rochester: 9–12 noon sponsored sin-in at Cathedral by Auxiliary Choir in aid of Wisdom Hospice Appeal.

C. Argent *(Evening Post)*

CORRECTION: WORLD WAR II has not ceased as advised on our last Bulletin.

C. Harfield *(Williams Bros. Bulletin)*

Close your eyes and stretch out your arms, and you are seven times more likely to touch someone in Luton than you are in the rest of the county.

G. Ridgewell *(Luton Evening Post)*

Augustus John the famous artist and portrait painter would most certainly have been a Haverfordwest boy had not his mother moved to beside the sea not long before he was born.

C. Belshaw *(Free Guide to Haverfordwest)*

Cairo Telephone List 1983 is now being compiled. If you wish to be included, please submit your family name, husband and wife's first name, address, district, telephone number (You do not need a telephone to be listed).

S. O'Neill *(Egyptian Gazette)*

THE
END
IS IN
SIGHT

GOOD NEWS BIBLE
USEFUL SERMONS
SONGS OF PRAISE

20

Women here live full and satisfying lives and people who live in council houses do not need these sex aids.

I. Griffiths (*Watford Observer*)

I'm a referee and no referee is 100 per cent perfect. You've only got two pairs of eyes.

C. Harbottle (*Fiji Sun*)

Mr Frank McDonald, RVBA president, said Bill Myers was a leading light in bowls for many years and his absence will be greatly missed.

A. Jones (*Bowls, Melbourne*)

Lothian Region's explanation? "It is not our policy to put a lamp standard in the middle of a footpath. That would be silly. Someone must have moved the wall."

D. Ritchie (*Glasgow Sunday Post*)

When the bomb drops, Eynsham will be ready! The parish council have appointed Mr K. J. Sheffield to liaise with Southern Electricity so that power can be restored quickly after a nuclear strike. Council chairman Mr David Wastie explained: "If any of the villagers notice anything unusual, they will alert Mr Sheffield and he will contact the electricity board."

C. Peat (*Oxford Star*)

The King Abdul Aziz International Airport in Jiddah is provided with the latest facilities such as run-ways.

D. Sandison (*Saudi Arabian Monetary Agency annual report*)

News of what God is doing in South Yorkshire. "MY LEG GREW FIVE INCHES."

R. Gaubert (*The New Life*)

BAKEWELL, DERBYSHIRE. The gateway to The Peaks, immortalized by its tarts.

D. Spooner (*Home and Country*)

The ambitious project for the village, known to generations as "God's own country" due to its addiction to Primitive Methodism and Horlicks, is the brainchild of the members of Alsagers Bank Wesleyan Youth Club (average age 68).

M. Paffard (*Newcastle Advertiser*)

A bus driver told a court that if he was disqualified from driving he would probably lose his job.

M. Ives-Lacy (*Newcastle Evening Chronicle*)

"As for the darts team, it is not true to say there will be no welcome for them—they are valued customers of many years standing. But it is true that there will not be a dart board after the alterations."

G. Gittins *(Stockport Messenger)*

Walmer Social and Educational Centre used the theme drama selections with members portraying characters from Romeo and Juliet, Anthony and Cleopatra and Worzel Gummidge (one of Shakespeare's more obscure plays).

M. Britton *(East Kent Mercury)*

Undertaker Michael Morris begins the task this week of injecting new life into Bideford Rugby Club.

S. Lock *(North Devon Journal Herald)*

HEAD BOUNCER Required for small market town discotheque in Bedfordshire. To work with 2 other doormen in this friendly, family atmosphere.

J. Higgins *(Yorkshire Evening Post)*

A HEALING SESSION By John Cain (of Birkenhead). Owing to illness: MEETING CANCELLED.

E. Fitton *(Southport Visiter)*

Allington Park Raceway presents ALL ACTION BANGER RACING plus Super Rods. Only £2 per car admission. If wet will be held in village hall.

D. Hall *(Southern Evening Echo)*

The technicians are working 24 hours—and sometimes more—per day to put the defective units back on stream and may even gain a little time on the dates projected.

C. Jasper *(Daily Gleaner, Kingston, Jamaica)*

A Christian gentleman was buried in Bloemfontein yesterday. The Prime Minister, Mr P. W. Botha said: "The life of Charles Robberts Swart was our most valued possession. His death leaves us richer."

K. Walton *(Rand Daily Mail)*

I would like to thank Mr Young for his concern and hard work towards the old and aged and all other Labour councillors.

A. Nuttall *(East Kent Mercury)*

The staff of a Kenton school is to be cut despite the fact that it will have more pupils. St Joseph's Infant School will lose half a teacher.

L. Engelhard *(Harrow Observer)*

23

"Dyson's catch of Clarke was unbelievable, the best catch I've seen! And the one before it was just as good."

T. Porter *(Sydney Daily Telegraph)*

Last August, a man was found wandering on the grounds claiming he was in love with Princess Anne. He was found to be mentally disturbed.

T. Sherman *(Washington Post)*

A Windermere woman's pet Yorkshire terrier was killed by a wild monk which leapt through a window and attacked it.

J. Airey *(North-western Evening Mail)*

The Ministry of Supply and Home Trade will put on the market 19,000 tons of meat and poultry to meet the increased consumption needs during the fasting month of Ramadan.

A. Singleton *(Egyptian Gazette)*

Mrs Reagan listens to speeches by her husband the pope.

R. LaVerriere *(Newport News Daily Press, Virginia)*

In a series of daring nighttime burglaries, thieves have stolen half the newly erected overhead street lights in the Umoja housing estate on the outskirts of Nairobi, the Kenyan News Agency said Monday. The street lights were put in place to cut down the number of nighttime burglaries in the area.

J. Pett *(Emirates News)*

It is embarrassing to observe the way in which the new mineworkers' president is behaving. Mr Scargill's brains appear to have gone to his head.

A. Purvis *(Wolverhampton Express and Star)*

Reading councillors have rejected a scheme to "adopt an animal" at a local zoo. Mr John Silverthorne said: "We might be sponsoring an expensive white elephant with this scheme."

B. Thorpe-Tracey *(Reading Chronicle)*

Mr Reagan sat between the Queen and her sister Princess Margaret Thatcher.

B. Shillitoe *(Majorca Daily Bulletin)*

They spent some time in London—and Switzerland—where Riding became interested in the creation of a movement to stop World War II. This was not successful.

J. Duley *(The Weekend Australian Magazine)*

LOST. Brown and black dog, has pie-balled left eye and limps, got half of right ear missing and no tail, answers to the name of Lucky.

M. Smith *(Huddersfield Examiner)*

I don't think the Royal baby should be called George. Every Tom, Dick and Harry is George. I think Jason would be a nice name.

W. Bartsch *(Melbourne Age)*

The Palace Theatre, Manchester, is delighted to announce that Van Morrison will give one concert only at the theatre on Monday evening.

S. Barber *(Sale & Altrincham Messenger)*

You are cordially invited to attend an Open House at Hummel Funeral Home.

T. Devine *(Akron Beacon-Journal, USA)*

Six dresses, two blouses, two skirts and two blue nighties, have been stolen from the men's drying room at Trinity and All Saints' Colleges at Horsforth, Leeds.

L. Rhodes *(Yorkshire Evening Post)*

What kind of society do we live in for one to stoop so low as to steal a hanging basket?

G. Knott *(Thanet Times)*

The New leader of Herts teachers is a woman who left school at 15 and is now a leading figure in schoolboys' wrestling.

Anon *(Hitchin Express)*

If the horse is not too lively, have the bridle slipped when it is still and ask the owner to move slowly away making a noise like a bag of oats.

J. Ammundsen *(What Camera Weekly)*

Organisers of a ten-mile "Jog for Jobs" to be held on Saturday are to stage a re-run on Sunday. The move follows a number of enquiries by people who are unable to make the run on the day because they are working.

T. Knott *(Pontefract and Castleford Express)*

Mr Andrew Macfarlane, defending, stressed Admirall's current financial difficulties. He owed £600 for textiles he had bought and sold at a loss, had to pay back a £400 personal loan, and has an overdraft of £250. In two weeks he will sit the finals of his four-year business studies degree course.

D. Vaughan *(Bath and West Evening Chronicle)*

R.I.P

ALF SCROGG

HAIRDRESSER

DUNTRIMMING

Sales of kangaroo meat in Japan are growing by leaps and bounds.

D. Warren-Knott *(Mainichi Daily News)*

Emma came up for the day to mark the launching of a new range of Peugeot cars. Mr David Langridge, director of the garage, said: "The emblem for Peugeot is a lion, so we thought a tiger would be a good idea."

G. Markham *(Peterborough Advertiser)*

"I wrote to him in Rome asking him to bless Bedford as he flies over and I had a very encouraging reply. I think he will probably do so . . . unless he makes a mistake and blesses Hemel Hempstead instead."

R. Lawton *(Bedfordshire On Sunday)*

Churchyard maintenance is becoming increasingly difficult and it will be appreciated if parishioners would cut the grass round their own graves.

B. Lacey *(Western Daily Press)*

The sex-shop provisions of the new Local Government Bill were tightened by the Lords last night to include hovercraft.

E. Marsh *(Sheffield Morning Telegraph)*

The Seychelles director of civil aviation admitted yesterday he had 15 minutes to prevent an Air India jet from landing in the middle of a coup attempt—but didn't because he was hiding under a desk with a dustbin over his head.

M. Thompson *(Zimbabwe Herald)*

HOPE FOR DEATH PENALTY GIVEN NEW LIFE.

A. Wareham *(Plattsburgh Press-Republican)*

The production of the play "World Without Men" was cancelled by the local Women's Institute last night. A spokesman explained every member of the cast—seven women and a cat—had become pregnant.

M. Mallory *(Washington Post)*

Millions of small birds had just left Britain for the warmer climates of an African winter. One of them was a willow warbler from Wolverhampton.

C. Millard *(Wolverhampton Express and Star)*

On the way out to the Middle East, he recalls, they travelled via the Cape on the Queen Mary, with 10,000 troops and 16 officers sharing a two-berth cabin.

D. Symons *(Canberra Standard)*

Estate agent, Steven Rotherham, who will handle the sale of the three separate houses, said he thought the two new smaller houses could be called simply Nos. 1 and 2 St Osyth's Cottages, but Mrs Valerie Green said that this could be a hazard for people who lisp.

S. Reed *(Bucks Herald)*

The Liberals are the party who tell you what's going on. Did anyone else provide you with copies of the new bus timetables?

M. Ives-Lacy *(Focus: Newsletter of Fawdon Liberal Association)*

The link between the distance an Austin Metro HLE can run on a single gallon of petrol, and thermal underwear for old age pensioners might be a mystery to most, but not to members of Knights Chapter (305) Angus, Perth and District Province of the Royal Antediluvian Order of Buffaloes.

R. Goddard *(Dundee Courier and Advertiser)*

Tiverton police were today looking for a man with pointed ears after the second case of indecent exposure in the last three days.

J. Cohen *(Exeter Express and Echo)*

Pittsburgh: The university here is investigating charges that under-graduates rolled and kicked seven human skulls on to a field before a rugby match, horrifying their opponents. Officials were said to be worried the incident might hurt the university's organ donor programmes.

P. Ward *(Glasgow Herald)*

Cypriot coffee is bitter, black and cinnamony. Not everybody's cup of tea.

B. Townley-Freeman *(Destination India)*

James Kearney was fined £35 at Hamilton Sheriff Court yesterday after admitting a breach of the peace by shouting and swearing at a cat near his home on January 15 and challenging it to a fight.

G. Haslie *(The Scotsman)*

If all the bumps in the High Street were ironed out, locals would have nothing on which to prop their bicycles warned Mr Charles Sayers at last week's meeting of Hurstpierpoint Parish Council.

M. Kennish *(Mid-Sussex Times)*

For tourists arriving and travelling in the USSR by air, rail or ship transfers on arrival and departure in each city on the itinerary are included in the cost of the tour for additional payment.

D. Crosby *(Soviet Union Holiday and Travel Guide)*

"Many church-goers are missing communion because there is no wine," he explained. "But if we are really remembering what our Lord has done, tea and biscuits would do and so wine made from mangoes is quite adequate."

A. Bateman *(Bedfordshire Times)*

The Vikings have been causing fainting fits in York, but they have also been making squirrels very happy.

I. Cochrane *(Yorkshire Post)*

A former mayor yesterday said allegations that he had kneed a man on an election day arose from a unique system of handing out how-to-vote cards.

L. O'Neill *(Melbourne Sun)*

When asked which country he was going to, Mr Leslie had replied "Pontins". This, said Mr Earlam, was an indication that his client was not very sophisticated.

I. Sergeant *(Runcorn Guardian)*

If a litter bin is provided at the lay-by on the A6 in Shardlow, near the turn off to The Wharf, it will attract rubbish, fears the parish council.

M. Osborne *(Long Eaton Advertiser)*

Two years ago Mrs Sheila MacDonald came home to find an Alfa Romeo in her front room. Six months ago it was a Ford Transit van. Yesterday it was a heavy goods lorry and a Renault.

M. Hewson *(Southern Evening Echo)*

St Patrick's Day got off to a flying start for the Irish national airline. Aer Lingus proudly displayed a model of one of their Boeing 737's at an Irish breakfast at a Midland hotel. But celebrations came down with a bump when an organiser spotted that the plane's wings were upside down.

R. Yates *(Birmingham Evening Mail)*

A mouth organist accused of begging told Brighton magistrates today it was impossible to play the mouth organ and ask people for money at the same time. Police withdrew the charge.

J. Martin *(Brighton Evening Argus)*

Air stewardesses have been warned that if they have surgery to improve their cleavage, their breasts could explode in flight. The US Medical Association says silicone implants to enlarge breasts can explode at high altitudes.

R. Bladen *(Manchester Evening News)*

AUTOMATIC 1300 Austin, K reg, long M.o.T., taxed Jan. '83, radio, woman, £300.

F. Archer *(Richmond and Twickenham Guardian)*

A woman threw her dog at a 17-year-old Newhall youth who exposed himself to her, magistrates at Swadincoate heard.

R. G. Smith *(Burton Mail)*

Our food and facilities are subject to constant, voluntary inspection by two veterinarians.

G. Redfern *(German Railways Quik Pik Menu)*

Palermo's public health office was ordered closed today on the grounds that it was insanitary.

M. Long *(Malta Times)*

Yellow lines could soon be painted on roads crossing common grazing land at Beverley in a fresh attempt to stop cattle straying.

I. Cochrane *(Yorkshire Post)*

PERSONAL. One year's membership of health club, less than half price, due to illness.

J. Lodge *(Huddersfield Daily Examiner)*

At 51, with a wife and three children, Major Coles (Rtd.) is not at all loony.

J. Millard *(Wolverhampton Express and Star)*

Now they are married, Mr and Mrs Briscoe always take bread pudding with them when they go to the cinema.

G. Ridgewell *(Harlow Star)*

The holes in the road are four inches deep, and I do my best each week by trying to fill them with the uneaten portions of rice pudding from Sunday lunch. But it is to no avail.

S. Keohane *(Chiswick and Brentford Gazette)*

But the Ministry of Defence now says it will maintain neutrality through agreeing to supply both sides with arms.

J. Leroguer *(Lloyd's List)*

The owner of a large house with many light-bulb holders has been checking single and double life bulbs. She found to her surprise that the double-life bulbs lasted approximately twice as long as the single-life ones.

R. Kaye *(Western Evening Herald)*

"It was tremendous last year to win the first men's international title. My aim this year is the double—to win both the men's and ladies' events."

W. Anderson *(Golf World)*

Among the crowd of guests who stood on Bristol dockside on a cold day this spring to watch Lord Beswick, the chairman of British Aerospace, arrive by toad to open the city's new Industrial Museum, there must have been quite a number who were less than convinced of the future popularity of the venture.

G. Huggett *(Gloucestershire and Avon Life)*

If toads are having problems with traffic there are a variety of ways to help them including road signs.

P. Dansie *(Natural World)*

Monday night is Gay Night at the Manhattan and a thoughtful District Council has strung fairy lights along this section of the Walkway to add to the cosmopolitan atmosphere.

M. King *(Scottish Field)*

A football match between prisoners at Nottingham Jail and a local amateur side was held up when the ball was stolen.

E. Kent *(Gloucestershire Echo)*

In a bizarre early morning burglary in Hayes villains breaking into the back of an electrical goods store panicked and fled when alarmed by noise by other people breaking in at the front.

H. Few *(West Middlesex Express)*

A spokesman for the Stewardship Committee said this week that the two million lapel badges which were distributed bearing the message "God loves a fiver" should have read "God loves a giver". The badges can be amended with felt pens.

M. Hunter *(The Coracle, Iona)*

SITUATIONS VACANT. Male masseuse required, full or part time.
S. Livingston *(Burton Mail)*

MUCH ABOUT EARTH STILL UNKNOWN, SAYS EXPERT
C. O'Connor *(Khaleej Times)*

Although this telephone booth is unique, it is quite typical of many others in the country.

P. Walker *(New Straits Times)*

BOYS STOLE FREE CATALOGUES

G. Ridgewell (*Potters Bar Press*)

A case against a Rhymney Valley man was adjourned for a month by Caerphilly magistrates. He is charged with being in possession of a pair of brown socks for use in connection with a burglary on January 6.

P. Williams (*South Wales Echo*)

Michael Murphy, defending, said it was a case of absentmindedness. He said his client admitted looking over his shoulder, but it was a habit he had acquired from working on a psychiatric ward.

D. Minors (*Sheffield Star*)

He also asked for 14 other offences to be taken into consideration and was told by Judge Harry Walker: "You committed a string of offences and for what—for fruit machines. It is plum crazy."

N. Watson (*Huddersfield Daily Examiner*)

Vandals may be among the few people who really appreciate what Milton Keynes is trying to do for them.

T. Hopkins (*Luton Evening Post*)

The average Barnet resident is 52.4 per cent female.

G. Ridgewell (*Potters Bar Press*)

The climber Chris Bonnington who conquered Everest has cancelled a talk at Clifton Hall, Rotherham, because of snow.

R. Goddard (*Yorkshire Post*)

It had been estimated that the restoration of the hotel's old people could be as high as £25,000.

M. Ward-Campbell (*Harrogate Herald*)

A man got in and said he wanted to go to Fifth Avenue, just off the Harrow Road. "On the way he explained that his wife had been carrying on with another man, and he was going to sort him out. Well, eventually the cab drew up and he went to the front door. A man answered and he hit him, then dashed back to the cab. It was only when they got to the end of the road, they realised it was Sixth Avenue, not Fifth."

G. Ridgewell (*Watford Evening Echo*)

BANK HOLIDAYS—Changing Dates. Eastern Monday (Freek Orthodox Church)

R. Kokkinov (*Cyprus Time Out*)

A thief stole a suitcase containing a suit, other clothes and an electric razor which was left near a car in Yardley Street, Brighton. A police spokesman said: "The thief is probably smart and clean-shaven."

E. Lambert (*Brighton & Hove Gazette*)

Singles Club. If you think that your social life couldn't possibly be any more boring than it already is, join the Ecclesall Twenties Club and we might prove you wrong!

E. Mountain (*Sheffield Star*)

Vivien Leigh and Clark Gable in the BBC blockbuster "Gone With The Mind", which is being shown in two parts, on Boxing Day and Sunday.

B. Hain (*Nottingham Evening Post*)

GLC transport chief Dave Wetzel is to look at London Transport's recruitment policy after two people claimed they were refused jobs because they were unemployed.

J. Arthur (*South London Press*)

He went to a branch of a building society nearby to carry out a hold-up, but when an assistant approached him, he opened an account instead.

R. Queralt (*Oxford Mail*)

Wanted—Potential Managers are required for City Bank. Persons between 25 and 30 with 40 years' experience.

E. Shipley (*Lloyds Bank The Dark Horse*)

The concert was a great success. Special thanks are due to the vicar's daughter who laboured the whole evening at the piano, which as usual fell upon her.

S. Carter (*Palm Leaves, Dubai parish magazine*)

BEAUTIFUL, new, unbreakable dentures, also guaranteed repair in 30 min.

G. Ridgewell (*The Scotsman*)

A 48-year-old mother believed she was in Wales looking for a lost cat on the day she committed a shoplifting offence in Keighley, magistrates heard on Tuesday.

A. Smith (*Keighley News*)

ONE ROOM WITH FULL BATH for an Indian to share with another who is rarely using.

A. Bridger (*Khaleej Times*)

Broseley's Women Against Boredom group is worried by declining attendances at its monthly meetings.

M. Hall (*Bridgnorth Journal*)

A meat pie sold two days after the recommended date by Robert Gale of Ashtead, contained "spots of mould" on the crust and not "a good crop of mould" as reported in this newspaper last week. We are happy to put the record straight.

F. Start (*Leatherhead Advertiser*)

Club operators know a box office hit when they see one—and that's why Jim Davidson appears in Luton for only one night tomorrow evening.

T. Hopkins (*Luton Evening Post*)

"I was okay, though," Terry grins, "the doc gave me a brain scan and they found nothing."

M. McFadden (*Australian Bulletin*)

Relax Massage. For you sir in Athens and Pireaus with atomic sauna and large Scandinavian telephones.

K. Shewan (*Athens News*)

The Tecopa pupfish was removed from the US Government's list of endangered species yesterday because there aren't any more.

M. Preston (*Toronto Globe and Mail*)

He said: "Sex is one of our most powerful tools. For many of our rituals we require a virgin of 17 summers. Unfortunately, it's getting more and more difficult to find them in Eltham these days."

J. Johnston (*Lewisham Mercury*)

Monday, November 16. Hang-gliding Club meeting, 12.30 pm, above South-side Bar.

P. Wallace (*Felix, Imperial College Union*)

One example of Mr Reay's lack of consideration, she claims, was promising a honeymoon in Austria while intending taking her to Leighton Buzzard.

S. Wayne (*Bath & West Evening Chronicle*)

RESEARCH POSITION IN CHEMICAL OCEANOGRAPHY. Send résumé and references to Professor G. J. Wasserburg, Lunatic Asylum, California Institute of Technology, Pasadena.

J. Wittenberg (*Nature*)

11.10 PARKINSON. Michael Parkinson with his weekend guests Ian Dury, Diana Dors and Arthur Scargill, plus more boring postcards.
J. Purser (*Birmingham Evening Mail*)

A clean-up of the surroundings and interior improvements are to be made at the morgue in Builth Wells. The move follows protests by a local councillor who claimed the building wasn't fit to be seen dead in.
W. Mills (*Mid Wales Journal*)

Local Planning Applications: J. S. Smith, change of use of mortuary to meat processing unit, Knott Lane.
T. Rigg (*Wharfedale Observer*)

The underground bunker at Inverness which will play a vital role in the event of a nuclear war is out of action—a victim of years of neglect and vandalism. "It's a scandal," said a man who visited it. "The place looks like a bomb has hit it."
M. Pye (*Aberdeen Evening Express*)

Liz, who moved to Horsham from Middlesex in April, recently became the nation's first class-one woman referee—following in the footsteps of husband Philip.
J. Unwin (*Horsham Evening Argus*)

A spokesman for the organisers said: "Those who are dead or hard of hearing should sit in the north transept."
N. Smale (*Durham News*)

The seaman, severely injured when the ship was three hours out, was taken to hospital and the hippopotamus removed.
B. Lacey (*Western Mail*)

Flower gardens, lamp-posts, railings, shelters of Victorian design, maybe even a bastard, could enhance both visually and environmentally what is already potentially an attractive area.
E. Rhodes (*Lynn News & Advertiser*)

Unilateral disarmament, Mr Nott said, is a one-sided business unless pressure is put on the Soviet Union to disarm as well.
J. Howley (*Oxford Mail*)

One of two men who pushed a Wolverhampton man through the plate glass window of an aquatic shop told police: "It's save a brick week."
K. Broad (*Shropshire Post*)

Jimmy Carter left a legacy which may yet turn sour in the mouths of those who rode to victory on it.

H. Fairlie *(Vancouver Sun)*

RENT FREE fully furnished self-contained flat in Surbiton offered to married couple in exchange for wife.

G. Baker *(Midweek Surrey Comet)*

A man set light to the door of his flat as a protest against Birmingham Council's failure to crack down on fire-raisers.

S. Collins *(Birmingham Mail)*

A man made a brief appearance before the magistrates at Uxbridge on Wednesday charged with failing to neglect his family.

J. Maling *(Hayes News)*

To those of you who think that the RNLI National Lottery is always won by someone else, take heart. The £250 prize in the twelfth draw was won by Mrs K. M. Street, of Leigh on Sea.

J. Bow *(Yachting Monthly)*

Said Cllr. Dowd, "I asked a footballer I know if he preferred Astroturf to grass and he said he didn't know as he'd never smoked Astroturf."

P. Webb *(South London Press)*

In order to be able to offer better services and for the convenience of our customers, we are pleased to announce the cancellation of the Arabian Express Service between Jeddah and Riyadh as of Tuesday 17th.

M. Greening *(Arab News)*

A 40-year-old man wearing a pair of brown swimming trunks only, indecently exposed himself to four Asian ladies on the towpath by Richmond Bridge at 6pm. The girls, all in their early 20s, were unable to get a good look at the man before he turned and fled.

R. Turner *(Richmond Herald)*

SEE-THROUGH STAFF. Attractive see-through persons required for northern suburbs restaurant.

J. Copeland *(Adelaide Advertiser)*

A man who murdered his first wife, today admitted murdering his second . . . because she nagged about him killing the first.

T. McCormick *(Glasgow Evening Times)*

"Smoking can kill you," she told a House subcommittee and teenagers who had gathered for a look. "And if you've been killed," exclaimed Ms Shields, "you've lost a very important part of your life."

E. Martelle *(Texas Tobacco Industry Newsletter)*

THE MANOR CENTRE. Owing to unforseen circumstances our course entitled "Predicting Your Future" has had to be cancelled.

G. Hamill *(Cambridge Evening News)*

The meeting then voted to support fox hunting. A spokesman for Cheam YCs said: "People at the meeting appreciated the fact that foxes had to be stamped out for their own good."

C. Hudson *(Sutton Borough Guardian)*

Explaining his idea, he added: "There are a good many sites in Stoke-on-Trent which have benefited as a result of rubbish being tipped on them."

L. Scott *(Staffordshire Evening Sentinel)*

There will be a salmon barbecue going all day at the Lodge restaurant at Sewell's Marina near Derby headquarters, with proceeds going to the Save the Salmon fund.

J. Mackenzie-Elliott *(Vancouver Sun)*

Inspector John Tolley, prosecuting, said the assault happened on a bus after Karia asked Mr Rahim: "Why are you sitting on my knee?"

B. Bishop *(Leicester Mercury)*

Griffithstown Junior School was designed to take 420 pupils. It now has 421 and is seriously overcrowded.

G. Meredith *(Western Mail)*

PALMERS will prepare your Wedding Reception to meet your personal requirements. Home-made wedding cages a speciality.

V. Thomas *(Bath Evening Chronicle)*

A Mayor and his VIP guests got a surprise the night they went back to the mayoral parlour—for trapped inside were 14 widows.

J. Hawgood *(Northern Echo)*

"This is an exciting, skilfully designed proposal that will inject vitality into an area that is ripe for redevelopment," he said. Mr Fagan said the building would look good from the footpath "because you can't see it."

J. Boas *(Melbourne Age)*

The Sunday Times will publish a Business Efficiency Supplement on August 30. To be considered for publication in the Supplement all copy must reach the Editor by not later than September 25.

A. Borg-Cardona (*Malta Sunday Times*)

Mai Thai Finn is one of the students in the programme and was in the centre of the photo. We incorrectly listed her name as one of the items on the menu.

P. Barber (*Auckland Star*)

Mr Mafayai explained that his Ministry did not keep its last December promise of opening the new Ibadan airport because its terminal buildings were yet to be completed. The delay was due to the non-inclusion of the terminal buildings in the original plan of the new airport.

P. Welborn (*African Business*)

"He considered he had received a very firm verbal invitation and that everything was signed, sealed and delivered—although nothing was on paper."

D. Ritchie (*Dundee Courier and Advertiser*)

In a recent police call column, based on information given by Lerwick police station, it was stated that a pedestrian had been knocked down by a vehicle at Bixter. We have been asked to point out that the pedestrian was not knocked down, but was struck by the vehicle while lying on the road.

P. Tait (*Shetland Times*)

Solitude: Loneliness is a problem even among those who have been to school in Croydon.

M. Hawthornthwaite (*Croydon Advertiser*)

The video revolution that has been with us for the last decade has finally arrived.

B. Blackwell (*The Assistant Librarian*)

Thieves got away with two burglar alarms when they broke into a building site in Weir Road, Wimbledon. The alarms were on the outside wall of the buildings.

K. Tozer (*Wimbledon News*)

The only hiccup during a highly successful afternoon surrounded the boys' skipping race which had to be re-run when it was discovered one of the competitors was a girl.

N. Pendlebury (*Hampshire Chronicle*)

APOLOGY. Due to a typographical error in last week's issue of the Enfield Independent, the words "Con-Men" appeared on the border of Ashley & Nephews advertisement. "Con-Men" was the headline of a story that was not used because of lack of space and is absolutely nothing to do and is in no way connected with Ashley & Nephews. We apologise for any inconvenience or embarrassment caused by this unfortunate error and would like to make it clear that Ashley & Nephews are a well established and highly respectable company and are North London's largest suppliers of aids for the disabled.

J. Lambie (*Enfield Independent*)

Prison authorities in Oklahoma forgot to execute double murderer James White and yesterday he was granted a reprieve. White, 24, who has appealed against execution, said: "I remembered, but I wasn't going to say anything."

J. Thom (*Scottish Daily Record*)

A sheriff ruled yesterday that a stomach X-ray produced in court was inadmissible evidence because it had been obtained without a search warrant.

D. Gibson (*The Scotsman*)

Station inspector Donald Swanepoel said he was busy in his office awaiting the late passenger train when he heard a car travelling at high speed and then people screaming on the platform. Outside he saw a new car with all four of the wheels in the air and the axles resting on the railway lines. He did not like it because last year his station took the award for the neatest station in the area.

O. McGee (*Durban Daily News*)

According to one recent report two local women walking their dogs were startled by a naked man who leapt out at them. They managed to defend themselves with their car keys.

J. Scott (*Esher News and Mail*)

"Owning a car has become a very expensive business," he said. "The only time I use it is to take it round the corner to get petrol."

S. Evans (*Birmingham Evening Mail*)

BRIDE SHOPS. Even Lady Diana would look good in one of our range of dresses.

M. Mander (*Sutton Coldfield News*)

EASTER BUNNY SPECIAL. 15% off on Rabbit Meat.

J. Corrie (*The Press, British Columbia*)

A massive traffic jam clogged the centre of Belfast yesterday because Government officials were carrying out a survey to try to end rush-hour congestion.

T. Holyoake *(Derby Evening Telegraph)*

ATV. 9.40 Something Different: A repeat of Monday evening's programme.

R. Madden *(Leicester Mercury)*

We assure fluency in English in two months. British School of Language. Staff: trained by foreign mission. Method: Microwave.

Q. Grosberg *(Times of India)*

About 5,900 homeless men passed through Camberwell Reception Centre in the year ending July 1980. The Consortium Joint Planning Group has published a report which examines the impact on Southwark, Lewisham and Lambeth of the Centre's proposed closure by the DHSS in four years' time. "What homeless single people have in common," says the report, "is that they are single and homeless."

D. Finch *(London Housing)*

The band struck up on top of one of the buildings at 6 a.m. for 15 minutes before an angry headmaster, Mr John Phillips, unplugged the amplifiers in his dressing gown but said afterwards there would be no hard feelings as long as he got an apology.

J. Jones *(Oxford Mail)*

FOR SALE. One Large Headmaster answers to the name Jock house trained £10 or near offer.

J. Currie *(Merseymart)*

Mr Swann had shrapnel injuries to both eyes, but took part in the withdrawal from Blackpool, walking for three days through dense jungle and over high hill ranges in the monsoon.

C. Ramsey *(Leicester Mercury)*

Members of the Social Club are having a day out with a difference on Saturday. For members of the club are travelling to Arrochar for breakfast—and then to Rothesay to take part in a mixed promiscuous match at a local bowling green.

D. Buirski *(Hamilton Advertiser)*

RECORD LOSS ON THE BUSES. £3.5m deficit caused by improved services.

B. Mattimore *(Henley Times)*

Those of us who saw the return of the space shuttle on television must surely have linked this marvel of technology to the role of the Welfare Officer.

W. Martin *(Welfare & Social Services Journal)*

Mouzo was arrested and taken to Farnham police station, where he tried to kick his cell door—but he used both feet at the same time and fell over.

A. Bormick *(Farnham News and Mail)*

As part of a project on infant care, students have to simulate parenthood by taking care of a hard-boiled egg for a week.

P. Lowe *(Newsweek)*

Mr Lloyd says the train is being taken off because, among other reasons, it's too crowded.

T. Coello *(Swindon Evening Advertiser)*

A 4kg female salmon found 122km up the estuary of the Thames at Chertsey—the first to appear so far upstream since 1833—is yet another sign of Thames Water's success in cleaning the river. The fish was found dead between the bridge and the weir by a passerby.

J. O'Donohue *(Surveyor)*

Facts are hard to come by but I am sure that there is some truth in the reports. I am concerned that the British Medical Association should state categorically that it deprecates the activities of unscrupulous members of our profession who are out for a quick kill, at the expense of the reputation of the rest of us.

G. Noble *(British Medical Journal)*

The New South Wales Corrective Services Commission chairman, Dr Tony Vinson, will investigate a report that prisoners at Sydney's Parramatta gaol have access to women, drugs, alcohol and Chinese meals.

G. Arandelovic *(Adelaide Advertiser)*

HAMILTON (Canada): An American nudist in town to promote the Miss Nude world pageant being held in nearby Flamborough, Ontario, in July, was robbed of her costumes on Thursday.

S. Tiwari *(The Statesman)*

Film producer Greg Smith hopes to gross at least £10,000,000 from his film on the life of the penniless Percy French, the Roscommon-born song-writer, entertainer, musician and drains inspector.

P. Mason *(Irish Independent)*

He said it was pure theory to claim that a nuclear attack would mean the end of Chalfont St Peter.

A. Stacey (*Bucks Examiner*)

A pre-emptive nuclear strike, an outbreak of plague, or a major earthquake could all pose serious problems for Crediton Town Council if they occur in the next three months.

C. Oram (*Exeter Express*)

For jolly wearin'-o'-the green, the place to be on March 17 is Waikiki for the St Patrick's Day Parade, when more than 1,000 Irishmen—regardless of race, creed, or national origin—march down Kalakaua Avenue.

J. Ruddell (*Western's World*)

Letter and parcel-sorting in Sheffield is to be modernised during the next 12 months. Services should be unaffected.

F. Soar (*Sheffield Morning Telegraph*)

In fact, although this was the third meeting organised at the Airport this year by the Southern Autosport Association, not one other car has rolled, and despite the presence of the Emsworth Division, St John Ambulance Brigade, no drivers have been injured either.

D. Frost (*Portsmouth News*)

Lunch as packed by Mrs Kitchen for local primary schools: sausage roll, tomato, crisps and mouse.

A. Whatmore (*Lincolnshire Chronicle*)

Sir Roger Manwood's Grammar School, Sandwich, founded in 1563, will go educational in September next year.

L. Rylands (*Kent Messenger*)

BACH: ST MATTHEW PASSION (11.25 a.m.) is in two parts extending up to 4.40 and interrupted only by snooker.

P. Mason (*Dublin Evening Press*)

One man was stabbed and others were injured when violence again brought soccer to the people of Aston at the weekend.

E. Scott (*Birmingham Evening Mail*)

Menus in the Commons dining rooms will be printed in English and not French in future. Potages and consommes become soup and chips so all MPs can understand.

C. Machin (*Southend Evening Echo*)

Meat worth a total of £34 was stolen when thieves broke into the deep freeze in the garage of Mr T. Bone, at Woodside, Ashby-de-la-Zouch.

D. Gibbons *(Leicester Mercury)*

Residents of a Dun Laoghaire street who were warned to boil water which contained "tadpoles" today reported that they had done so. The "tadpoles", which were green, turned orange.

P. Mason *(Dublin Evening Press)*

Only two countries, France and Germany, have so far been put forward for twinning, and the council's Chief Executive, Mr Rodney Dew, virtually ruled out France because of a language barrier.

F. Lopey *(Woking News and Mail)*

God's Word says, "He that asks, receives" (Matthew 7:8). Jesus will answer if you believe. Try it. Phone 726-4797. Ask for Ivan.

J. Munro *(Melbourne Sun)*

M.O.T. While you wait (5 days).

C. Monson *(Rotherfield Friday Advertiser)*

In the evening in the main hall, there will be a dance/ceilidh with the Kilmory Girls who have graciously reformed for this performance.

E. Alderson *(Arran Banner)*

For a few hours, as President Ronald Reagan lay under the surgeon's wife, there appeared to be confusion. Who's running the country?

S. Roy *(Turkish Daily News)*

Bastions of British male society: the smoking room of the "Army and Nancy Club".

P. Lewis *(Die Welt)*

FIND-A-FRIEND AGENCY. Ages 18–30 years. Special concessions for Senior Citizens.

W. Mills *(Dover Express)*

The first mass rally of the new Committee of Citizens for Action Now was postponed last night for lack of a quorum.

R. Brooker *(Jerusalem Post)*

Mr Phillips had allowed the men to run a blue movie for an hour in working time, to sunbathe and swim in the River Frome and to hold card schools. He said: "It was the only way to get them to work."

J. Akroyd *(Shropshire Star)*

PRE-MARRIAGE COURSES begin April 26 & 28. Apply: College of Industrial Relations, Sandford Road, D6.

C. Mitchell *(Dublin Southside Express)*

He said the workshop answered a number of questions from participants, including general health subjects and how to tie up a lover without cutting off his circulation.

M. McCarthy *(San Francisco Chronicle)*

If the reader signing himself "Homeless" will let us know his full name and address—not for publication—we will be pleased to give space to his letter.

J. Judge *(Glasgow Evening Leader)*

"I find it astonishing that those residents who are quick to come along to collect free bus travel tokens cannot show their faces for the annual meeting. It would only take a minute for them to get into their cars and drive to the public car park across the way."

M. Chase *(West Sussex County Times)*

Skinhead Simon McMorrow, who leapt up and ripped a geranium out of a window sill display on County Hall, Chelmsford was doing its fellow flowers a service, Chelmsford magistrates heard on Monday. "In his considered opinion," said Mr Bill Brown, defending, "it was somewhat wilted and to all intents it was dead and he was doing its fellows a favour by removing it."

C. Porter *(Essex Weekly News)*

Communion wine was taken and an attempt made to open the vestry safe. Mr Percival said: "It was a very amateurish job. They spent some time breaking the door—but it was already open."

S. Brierley *(Bradford Telegraph & Argus)*

Motor accidents have replaced falling out of coconut trees as the most common cause of death in the Pacific islands.

D. Davies *(The Courier)*

A "politics mad" councillor who was injured in a motor-cycle accident was helped out of a coma by listening to taped speeches by David Steel and other Liberal leaders.

T. McCormick *(Glasgow Herald)*

A man who could neither read nor write was found guilty of forging cheques by Sandbach Magistrates on Wednesday.

L. Wakefield *(Crewe Chronicle)*

The annual oyster fishing season got under way in Tralee Bay, off Fenit yesterday with more than a 100 per cent drop in the number of boats.

Rev. W. Jones *(Irish Times)*

Police have not released the name of the Mini driver, who was unhurt. The Mini was driven by Gladys Wesley, of Halesowen, who was not hurt.

N. Quiney *(Wolverhampton Express and Star)*

Zambia produced 609,294 tonnes of finished steel to maintain its position as the fifth largest producer of copper in the world.

R. Dunstan *(Commonwealth)*

Petroleum Development Oman's driving and vehicle safety committee are looking into the possibility of introducing milestones at regular intervals along PDO roads in the Interior. They accept the idea in principle, but have called for details of basic costs, distance between milestones and so on.

P. Plummer *(Al Fahal)*

Asked by the magistrate why he spoke with an American accent when he was born and raised in South Africa and had never visited the United States, Mr Matthe replied that he stayed with a white family who were Scottish.

D. Durden *(Salisbury Herald)*

A County Donegal man killed in Iraq was recently prevented by bad weather from travelling to Ireland to visit members of his family.

P. O'Driscoll *(Irish Evening Press)*

For his contribution to community relations, Constable Albert Bailey was commended, as were Constables Gary Currie and Neil McKenna, responsible for numerous robberies on elderly women.

J. Williams *(Liverpool Daily Post)*

SITUATION VACANT. Teacher. Wanted Teacher for English for a leading secretarial college, part-time, English speaking an advantage, excellent prospects.

J. Frith *(Nairobi Standard)*

They will not be liable for any loss occasioned by any omission or misprint in the reproduction of any advertisement howsoever such omission or misprint howsoever such omission or misprint may be caused.

S. Seaton *(Wolverhampton Express and Star)*

Wimborne Juvenile Court heard yesterday that two schoolboys, said to have a special interest in churches, wrecked St Hubert's Parish Church at Corfe Mullen.

D. Garwood *(Bournemouth Evening Echo)*

VOLUNTEERS NEEDED for Marina Creations for cutting, assembling and visiting disabled persons.

L. Delaquerrière-Richardson *(London Free Press, Ontario)*

Newsletter 286 contained an item describing the renovations on the main floor of the Administration Building. "Wall has been removed" should, of course, have read "A wall has been removed". We apologise to Dr Wall, whose office is in this area, for any inconvenience he may have experienced as a result of this error.

Anon *(University of Manitoba Faculty Association Newsletter)*

West Dorset District Council's Personal Standing Committee have decided that it would not be practical to impose a total ban on smoking in their offices. They are considering, however, the possibility of prohibiting smoking in offices occupied entirely by non-smokers.

D. Ellis *(Dorset Evening Echo)*

Motions calling for the temporary suspension of capital punishment in Harrow's middle and high schools were on the agenda for the meeting of the borough education committee on Tuesday evening.

D. H. Robbins *(Harrow-Wembley Independent)*

Rpad sogms om Troubridge Crescent and Troubridge Avenue are confusiong and the community council would like to see these made more clear.

A. Bennie *(Paisley and Renfrewshire Gazette)*

But though a pathologist report showed that all three people who died in the Cortina were under the influence of drink he did not suspect they had been drinking.

C. Jackson *(Ilford Midweek Extra)*

Miss Jenny Wilson, manageress of The Epicurean Delicatessen in Market Street, said: "Our trade was about one third down. We had absolutely nobody in the shop all morning."

J. Butterworth *(Oxford Mail)*

Nothing could be further from the truth, apart from the fact that world-wide statistics have failed to prove that hanging is an effective detergent.

P. Martin *(Kingston and Surrey Guardian)*

A move is being considered to ban driving instructors from listening to music the headphones way, while giving lessons to learner drivers.

M. Wise *(Straits Times)*

Phase one of the multi-million pound scheme is due to start in 1986/87 but the preparatory work will be carried out later.

R. McGee *(Ormskirk Advertiser)*

A Bulawayo businessman told the city's High Court yesterday that in an alleged $20 million currency deal he was expected to hand the cash over to a man in a hotel bar wearing a white suit and a pale shirt and singing Baa Baa Black Sheep.

G. Carlisle *(Salisbury Herald)*

But what he describes as a significant and interesting finding is that breast-fed babies consult their doctors less often than bottle-fed babies.

J. Ritchie *(Glasgow Herald)*

An Australian diplomat, asked if his government fears an expansion of Russian influence in the area, responded: "Ha ha. Oh, ha ha ha. Well . . . oh, ha ha ha."

J. Cutcher *(Knoxville News-Sentinel)*

He said the annual balance sheet is now prepared annually instead of quarterly as it used to be before the Second World War.

S. Dickinson *(Heckmondwike Herald)*

The 28-year-old Whangarei solo mother, Suzie Green, gave birth to a 323-kilogram daughter Cinnamon.

L. Carr *(New Zealand Herald)*

From July all buses from Loughton Garage will be single deckers, explained Mr Brewer. This would keep down the garage overheads.

J. Caslaw *(West Essex Gazette)*

He agreed with Mr Craik that at the time of the robbery the company had a bank overdraft of around £170,000, owed creditors £599,892, and faced a trading deficit for the year of £267,000. But he said that in his opinion the firm were not in any serious financial difficulties.

A. Sutherland *(Glasgow Herald)*

A message in a bottle thrown into the sea nearly 23 years ago at Winterton has been found at Winterton.

R. Chappell *(Eastern Daily Press)*

32-year-old male wishes to meet female car owner in return for love and affection. Photo of car appreciated.

G. Ridgewell *(Hitchin Comet)*

"Wherever you get a crowd you get pickpockets. There have been one or two thefts at Cakwell and we are appealing to the fans to help themselves."

D. Bogg *(Rotherham Star)*

CARPETS Dirty, Muldy, Moth or any damages will be ruin your carpet. Call 5-726594, 5-734108, we will tell you how to do it.

R. Pilling *(South China Morning Post)*

A Harlow man running away from the police, hid under a car, but was soon caught because it was parked in a police station yard, Chelmsford Crown Court heard.

G. Ridgewell *(Harlow Gazette)*

RADIO. 9.15 Kruik-Blaasoktet—Octet for Two Oboes, Two Clarinets, Two Horns and Two Faggots, Op 103 by Beethoven.

I. Macdonald *(Durban Daily News)*

The Princess of Wales flew back to Balmoral after a visit south yesterday, accompanied by four Scots wearing plastic eyeballs on the end of springs.

P. Bannatyne *(Glasgow Herald)*

HAIR STYLIST, minimum 5 years experience on Corporation bus route.

C. Talbot *(East Essex Gazette)*

The Scottish Development Agency has this week announced it is to spend £9 over the next three years in a bid to create 650 local jobs. Now that may be good news for the valley but let's just pause for a moment and think.

S. Newton *(Ardrossan and Saltcoats Herald)*

After being arrested for fighting outside the Waterloo Hotel, Bacup, two men asked to be put in the same cell so they could finish the fight, Rossendale magistrates heard on Monday.

P. Macdonald *(Rochdale Observer)*

Donnelly was also charged with attempting to administer poison to Carmen Donnelly on September 26, with intent to annoy her.

T. Johns *(Sydney Sun)*

The reality may be something else. It may have been described for me by David Chassman, an MGM executive, the last time I was in Hollywood. "Conceding that we make movies only for 14-year-olds, 14-year-olds are interested in a lot more things than other 14-year-olds," he said. "We could do worse than make movies about all the things a 14-year-old is interested in."

B. Wolf *(Boston Globe)*

A walrus which has been cruising up and down the east coast of Britain for the past week looking for Greenland has finally been caught.

G. Ridgewell *(Watford Evening Echo)*

SCHIZOPHRENIC KILLED HERSELF WITH TWO PLASTIC BAGS.

P. Barnes *(Milton Keynes Gazette)*

FOR SALE. Steel Car Box Trailer. Ideal for dogs or musicians.

P. Dempster *(Cork Examiner)*

A crinkle-cut chip which just missed the dustbin and landed in a flower bed has taken root and become a potato plant at the home of Bryan Tones in Dudley.

V. Fox *(Yorkshire Evening Post)*

In a recent edition of your paper there was a long quotation from a Councillor Taylor. Then last week a Conservative candidate took umbridge about Councillor Taylor's comments. Who is "Councillor Taylor." Michael Danvers, Harlow.

You may well ask. First, could we correct your own mistake? The original quote was attributed to Councillor Turner, not Councillor Taylor. Councillor Turner became Councillor Taylor when Mr Hayes, the Conservative candidate, wrote to us with a reply. But Councillor Taylor does not exist. Neither does Councillor Turner—he was a figment of somebody's bad handwriting. The person in question is actually Councillor Smith.

G. Ridgewell *(Harlow Gazette)*

During the course of a sermon at the annual Mass for the repose of the soul of General Michael Collins at St Augustine's Church, Cork, last week, a man left the body of the church and walked to the pulpit apparently to remonstrate with the priest on the sermon's content. He was identified as the murdered Lord Mayor of Cork.

J. Andrychowski *(Cork Weekly Examiner)*

Thames shads, flounders, eels and whitebait were caught for food, and over one million lamperns were sold annually to Dutch fishermen for use as bait. Even the occasional surgeon was taken in the tideway.

M. Evans *(Merseyside Mercedo News)*

Borders Regional Council invite applications for the following: CAREERS OFFICER (UNEMPLOYMENT SPECIALIST).

I. Alexander *(Glasgow Herald)*

A little over half of the marriages in Kent last year (52 per cent) took place in register offices—which also means that many of the married couples chose to marry in church.

J. Dobson *(Tunbridge Wells News in Focus)*

On the following day, Paul Robinson will perform "Perambulation for Violin" and "Sonata for Violin, Piano and Two Tomato Sandwiches".

C. Manners *(North West Artful Reporter)*

But a palace spokesman, who in accordance with British practice declined to be named, refused to comment.

F. Illig *(San Diego Tribune)*

Every time a Cheltenham woman cleaned her shoes with Reckitt and Colman polish, her television changed channels—usually to ITV.

K. Kent *(Hull Daily Mail)*

Steve Gittins and his wife were told they could not have a cut in rates because they have a "wonderful view of Luton." But to enjoy the view Mr Gittins has to stand on a chair in his small garden and peer over the fence.

G. Ridgewell *(Luton Evening Post)*

Vauxhall Motors lost £59,887,000 in first six months 1981. Compares with large carving knife still in her back. Neighbours heard net loss of £7m in first half last year.

A. Farmer *(Swindon Evening Advertiser)*

HEAVY DRINKING BLAMED FOR ALCOHOLISM.

Anon *(Times of Zambia)*

Smith and Young returned carrying the three foot long bars. When questioned by the police they claimed they had the bars for self defence. Both men later said this wan't true. Young said: "We were messing about sword fighting."

G. Ridgewell *(Watford Evening Echo)*

TUDOR RESTAURANT. Trevor and Manola wish to thank customers for their kind support during 1981 and we are now taking bookings for your Christmas Parties and Dinners. Closed from 20th December—1st February.

R. Morton *(Lakeland Echo)*

BBC2 6.00 NEWS REVIEW: Plus a visual commentary for the blind.

B. Earl *(Sheffield Star)*

Mrs Brenda Woodhouse, of Cottingham, appeared before South Hunsley magistrates and was ordered to keep her Afghan under proper control. Chairman Mr Jack Barker told Mrs Woodhouse: "With a name like yours you ought to be able to keep it under control."

E. Kent *(Hull Daily Mail)*

Homicide Squad police have counted 64 stab wounds in the body of Mr Gerald Cuthbert, a New Zealander, whose body was found in a Paddington flat yesterday. They suspect it was not suicide.

L. Ellison *(Sydney Morning Herald)*

A driver who assaulted his wife after she had boarded the bus he was driving was fined £25 at Greenock yesterday. David Brabson, 31, was fined an additional £45 for a breach of the peace when he tried to commit suicide.

B. Horne *(Glasgow Daily Record)*

FOR SALE. Bunk beds complete with mattresses only £25. Also dining table and 4 chairs in white, ideal for 4 people only £25.

S. Lord *(Godalming Times)*

The Australian airline Quantas has denied one of its 747SP aircraft missed a hill on an approach to Wellington airport yesterday.

J. Redshaw *(Otago Daily Times)*

A tortoise had to have plastic surgery on its shell after a 14-year-old schoolboy shot it with an air rifle. But the incident was a mistake, Preston Juvenile court was told today. The boy had intended to shoot the neighbour's cat.

P. Rainford *(Lancashire Evening Post)*

Police said that a fire was found burning next to the body but they still do not know the cause. The car too was slightly burnt. The dead man was putting on a khakhi trousers and a pair of brown shoes when he was found.

M. Kent *(Botswana Daily News)*

WOMAN IN TRAIN FALL ALMOST UNHURT.

G. Ridgewell (*Watford Observer*)

"Well, when they (BILD officials) tell me we have 82 projects or some such number under way, six more than when we announced the plan, and 38 or 39 or 40 or 50 or whatever is the right number have had some degree of action or approval, not all of which have had funds, then I can only tell you we know where we are in every one of those." He said he couldn't vouch for the accuracy of the figures, which he said he had cited "off the top of my head".

J. McSherry (*Canadian Whig-Standard*)

Keith Tasker was upset when somebody sneaked on him for trying to deceive a loan company, Hull magistrates were told. "You can't trust anyone these days," he told police after he was arrested.

E. Kent (*Hull Daily Mail*)

In Fordsburg, Johannesburg, the two SAIC candidates were running neck-and-neck after two hours of polling—they had received one vote each. Mr Nanubhai Desai voted for himself and Mr Haroom Mayet voted for his father, Mr I. F. H. Mayet. There are nearly 4,000 voters in the constituency.

J. Mervis (*Johannesburg Star*)

"A schoolboy's head had become stuck in a vase. His mother was rushing him off to hospital. Presumably in order to avoid attracting attention, she had placed her son's school cap on top of the vase."

B. Lacey (*Western Daily Press*)

10. TOGETHER TONIGHT. Human interest magazine program about Melbourne. Featuring Greg Evans, Kerry Armstrong, Louise Philip, Andrew Harris. Tonight's stories include an interview with Captain Mark Phillips, the world's smallest mountain, interview with Jacki Weaver and John Waters and Scruff the singing dog.

S. Fraser (*Melbourne Herald*)

His friends will be sorry to learn that he had an operation last Wednesday and had his leg removed. All going well he should be back on his feet by the end of November.

R. Zanelli (*Cobar Age, New South Wales*)

A third member of the security firm was also in the shop, but could not give evidence, Mr Mayhew told the court, because he was currently serving a prison sentence.

P. Linton (*Hexham Courant*)

The town seems to be full of aimless, disorientated, strolling, lost, bewildered, bored, immobile, giddy, confused and wandering tourists, shoppers, women and other degenerates.

B. leBail (*Jersey Evening Post*)

The weather service had to dispatch employees to read its Civic Center rain gauge after an automatic gauge failed because of the rain, said Bob Webster, a weather service spokesman.

D. Westheimer (*Los Angeles Times*)

Eight Welsh Labour MPs have been given places in Michael Foot's seven-strong Front Bench team which was announced yesterday.

C. Jeanes (*Western Mail*)

This week Nicola Jones, an 18-year-old catering student, was chosen to represent Southport in the Catermind Student 1982 contest. Nicola goes forward to the heats at Hollings College, Manchester, in February, and if successful will be grilled by Magnus Magnusson in the London finals in May.

G. Deering (*Southport Visiter*)

A Japanese company is to build Britain's first completely unmanned factory in Worcester. Although the principal aim of this multi-million pound investment would be to buy computer-controlled machine tools to manufacture machine components, the factory could provide up to 500 new jobs.

J. Harvey (*The Engineer*)

Returning from a German holiday, Agnes Martin called police when she suffered a severe asthma attack in her car on the M20 at Leybourne. Mrs Martin was taken to West Malling police station, where there was an agonising waie the ct, whilontinental plug on her electric whaler was charged.

J. Page (*Kent Messenger*)

What do Tiddenfoot Leisure Centre and the Space Shuttle have in common? They have both been put out of action by loose tiles.

D. Dell (*Beds and Bucks Observer*)

Stevie of Southsea. January Sale begins Thursday this week November 26.

K. Frith (*Portsmouth News*)

About half the 2200 strikers at the state-owned company's Longbridge plant in Birmingham decided unanimously to stay out.

R. Nairn (*Melbourne Herald*)